Navigating the New Frontiers of Mental Health AI, Trauma, and Digital Wellness

BY ALAN SAUNDERS

This book is intended for informational purposes only.
The advice and strategies contained herein may not be
suitable for every individual, and the author and
publisher disclaim any liability or responsibility for any
loss or damage resulting from the use of this material.
While every effort has been made to ensure the accuracy
of the information provided, the author and publisher
make no representations or warranties regarding the
completeness, accuracy, or applicability of the content to
your particular situation.
First published 08/2024.
Printed and bound in the United States.

Thank You for Your Purchase!

Dear Reader,

Thank you for choosing *Navigating the New Frontiers of Mental Health AI, Trauma, and Digital Wellness*!

I'm thrilled to have you here and hope the insights into the new frontiers in mental health AI within these pages will prove valuable to you.

And when you've finished, if it's not too much trouble, I would greatly appreciate it if you could take a few moments to leave a review. Your feedback not only helps me improve but also serves as a guide for others who are considering whether this book might be right for them.

Thank you for your trust and support.

With gratitude,

Alan Saunders

Table of Contents

The Evolution of Mental Health Care in the Digital Age

Introduction

The landscape of mental health care has undergone a significant transformation in recent years. What was once a domain primarily characterised by face-to-face therapy sessions and traditional medication regimens is now being reshaped by the digital revolution. Today, technology, particularly Artificial Intelligence (AI), plays an increasingly central role in understanding, diagnosing, and treating mental health issues. For young adults and parents alike, understanding these changes is crucial for navigating this new and evolving terrain. This chapter provides a comprehensive guide to the evolution of mental health care in the digital age, exploring the opportunities and challenges of this technological shift.

The Digital Shift: A New Era of Mental Health Care

Technology integration into mental health care has been a gradual but transformative process, marked by several key milestones that have paved the way for the AI-driven solutions we see today. One of the earliest and most impactful shifts was the advent of teletherapy—therapy sessions conducted via video calls. Initially adopted as a convenience, teletherapy quickly proved to be more than just an alternative to in-person sessions; it offered a more accessible and flexible option for those who found it challenging to attend face-to-face therapy due to geographical, physical, or time constraints.

Teletherapy allowed mental health care to reach a wider audience, particularly those in remote or underserved areas. The rise of online mental health resources further enhanced this accessibility. Websites, forums, and, later, mobile apps such as *Calm* and *Headspace* emerged, offering users tools to manage stress, anxiety, and other mental health challenges on their terms. These digital platforms democratised access to mental health care, empowering individuals to seek help when and where they needed it, often without the stigma that can be associated with traditional mental health services.

However, the proliferation of these digital resources also brought new challenges. The quality of care varied widely across different platforms, and concerns quickly arose about the lack of personal connection that traditional therapy provided. While teletherapy maintained the personal interaction between therapist and patient, many online tools and apps offered a more impersonal experience, which could lead to feelings of isolation or inadequacy in users who needed more direct support.

This is where AI began to play a more prominent role, promising to bridge these gaps by providing more personalised, data-driven approaches to mental health care. AI's ability to analyse vast amounts of data in real-time has opened up new possibilities for early diagnosis, customised treatment plans, and ongoing support, marking a significant evolution in the mental health care landscape.

The Role of AI: Beyond Automation

AI in mental health care is about much more than automating routine tasks; it can revolutionise how we approach mental health by offering insights and treatments tailored to individual needs. One of the most promising applications of AI lies in predictive analytics, where AI systems analyse vast datasets to identify patterns that may indicate a person is at risk of developing mental health issues long before symptoms become apparent.

For instance, an AI tool might analyse data from wearable devices, such as heart rate monitors and sleep trackers, as well as social media activity and speech patterns, to detect early signs of conditions like depression or anxiety. This predictive capability could enable earlier interventions, potentially preventing more severe mental health crises from developing. Imagine an AI system noticing that a person's sleep patterns have become irregular, their social media posts have taken on a more negative tone, and their physical activity levels have decreased. The AI could then alert the individual or their healthcare provider, prompting a timely intervention that might include changes in lifestyle, therapy, or even medical treatment.

Moreover, AI is being harnessed to develop chatbots like *Woebot* and *Wysa*, which provide users with real-time mental health support. These AI-driven tools engage users in conversations, offering cognitive-behavioural therapy (CBT) techniques, mindfulness exercises, and coping strategies. While these tools are not a replacement for professional care, they serve as valuable supplements, providing support between traditional therapy sessions and offering immediate assistance when needed. The use of AI in this way can help individuals manage their mental health more effectively, making care more consistent and responsive.

Case Study: The Impact of AI on Early Diagnosis

To illustrate the potential of AI in mental health care, let's consider the case of Emily, a 17-year-old high school student. Like many teenagers, Emily struggled with stress and anxiety, particularly as her final exams and college applications loomed on the horizon. Her parents noticed that she was becoming more withdrawn and irritable, but they attributed this to the typical pressures of senior year and did not initially consider seeking professional help.

However, Emily had been using a mental health app that incorporated AI to monitor her mood and behaviour. This app analysed her activity levels, sleep patterns, and even the tone of her voice in her journal entries. Over time, the AI detected a pattern that suggested Emily was at risk of developing depression. The app sent a notification, encouraging her to seek professional help.

Thanks to this early warning, Emily's parents were able to connect her with a therapist before her condition worsened. The therapist confirmed that Emily was indeed showing early signs of depression, and together, they developed a treatment plan that included both therapy and lifestyle changes, such as improving her sleep hygiene and incorporating regular physical activity into her routine. Emily's story highlights how AI can play a critical role in early diagnosis, potentially averting more serious mental health issues by enabling timely intervention.

The Ethical Landscape: Challenges and Considerations

While the potential benefits of AI in mental health care are significant, they come with a host of ethical challenges that must be carefully navigated. One of the primary concerns is privacy. Mental health data is among the most sensitive information a person can share, and AI raises questions about how this data is stored, analysed, and protected. In an era where data breaches are increasingly common, ensuring the confidentiality and security of mental health data is paramount.

Moreover, bias is an issue in AI algorithms. AI systems are only as good as the data they are trained on, and if this data is not diverse or representative, the AI may produce biased results that do not accurately reflect the needs of all users. For example, an AI tool trained primarily on data from white, middle-class users might not be as effective in identifying mental health issues in users from different racial, ethnic, or socioeconomic backgrounds. This could lead to misdiagnoses, ineffective treatments, or even the exacerbation of existing health disparities.

These ethical challenges highlight the need for careful oversight and regulation of AI in mental health care. As these technologies continue to evolve, it will be crucial to ensure that they are used ethically and equitably, serving the needs of all users rather than reinforcing existing biases or inequalities. This might involve the development of more diverse and inclusive datasets and the implementation of robust privacy protections and ethical guidelines to govern the use of AI in mental health settings.

The Broader Impact of AI on Mental Health Care

Beyond individual cases like Emily's, the broader impact of AI on mental health care is profound. AI has the potential to transform not only how we diagnose and treat mental health issues but also how we understand them on a societal level. For instance, AI can analyse population-level data, identifying trends and risk factors that might go unnoticed. This could lead to more effective public health interventions and a better understanding of the social determinants of mental health.

Furthermore, AI-driven tools can help reduce the stigma associated with mental health issues by making care more accessible and less intimidating. For some individuals, talking to a therapist might be daunting, but interacting with an AI chatbot in the privacy of their own home could feel like a less intrusive first step towards seeking help. Over time, as AI becomes more integrated into mental health care, it could help to normalise the conversation around mental health, encouraging more people to seek the support they need.

Conclusion

The digital revolution has brought about profound changes in mental health care, offering new tools and approaches that were unimaginable just a decade ago. AI, in particular, holds great promise for improving the accessibility, accuracy, and effectiveness of mental health care. However, as with any powerful tool, it must be used responsibly. As we move forward, it will be essential to balance innovation with ethical considerations, ensuring that technology enhances rather than diminishes the quality of mental health care. By understanding and navigating these changes, young adults, parents, and mental health professionals alike can better support their mental health and that of others in this rapidly evolving landscape.

AI in Mental Health: The Double-Edged Sword

Introduction

Artificial Intelligence (AI) is often hailed as the future of mental health care, offering solutions from early diagnosis to personalised treatment plans. However, as with any powerful technology, AI in mental health is a double-edged sword. While it holds immense potential to transform how we approach mental health care, it also presents significant risks and challenges. This chapter explores both sides of this technological revolution, providing young adults and parents with a balanced view of what AI can — and cannot — do for mental health.

The Promise of AI: Revolutionising Mental Health Care

At its core, AI is about making sense of vast amounts of data. In the context of mental health, this means analysing everything from medical records and genetic information to social media activity and wearable device data. AI can identify patterns that might be invisible to the human eye, offering insights that lead to earlier and more accurate diagnoses.

Enhancing Diagnosis and Treatment

AI's ability to process and analyse large datasets allows it to detect subtle indicators of mental health conditions that traditional methods might overlook. For instance, AI can examine an individual's speech patterns, tone of voice, and even the speed of their speech to identify signs of depression or anxiety. This level of analysis can lead to more precise diagnoses and, consequently, more effective treatment plans.

Moreover, AI can help tailor these treatment plans to individual needs. Traditional mental health care often relies on a trial-and-error approach, where different therapies or medications are tried until the right combination is found. However, AI can streamline this process by predicting which treatments are most likely effective based on a person's specific data. This could significantly reduce the time it takes patients to find relief from their symptoms, improving overall outcomes.

Real-Time Support and Crisis Prevention

AI-driven tools like *Ginger* and *Mindsense* are already in use, providing real-time mental health support. These platforms analyse user data to offer personalised advice and coping strategies, helping individuals manage stress, anxiety, and depression more effectively. By continuously learning from each interaction, these AI systems become increasingly adept at tailoring their responses to the unique needs of each user.

One of the most exciting applications of AI in mental health is its potential to predict mental health crises before they happen. Research has shown that AI can analyse factors such as changes in sleep patterns, social interactions, and even speech patterns to predict when someone might be at risk of a mental health crisis. This predictive capability could be a game-changer in preventing severe outcomes such as suicide, relapse into addiction, or severe depressive episodes. By alerting patients and their caregivers to potential risks, AI can enable timely interventions that might save lives.

Case Study: AI in Action—Preventing a Crisis

Consider the story of Jason, a college sophomore who has been struggling with depression since high school. Despite regular therapy sessions and medication, Jason's mental health continued to decline. His parents were worried but unsure of what to do next.

Jason began using an AI-powered mental health app that tracked his daily activities, mood, and social interactions. Over time, the app detected subtle changes in Jason's behaviour—he was sleeping less, interacting less with friends, and his journal entries had a darker tone. The AI flagged these changes and sent Jason and his therapist an alert.

This early intervention allowed Jason's therapist to adjust his treatment plan, incorporating more intensive therapy sessions and a review of his medication. Jason's parents were also notified and were able to provide additional support during this critical period. Thanks to the AI's timely alert, a potential crisis was averted, and Jason's mental health began to improve.

Jason's case illustrates the profound impact that AI can have on mental health care. By providing real-time monitoring and predictive insights, AI can help prevent crises and ensure that individuals receive the support they need when they need it most.

The Risks of AI: Privacy, Bias, and Dependence

Despite the promise of AI in mental health care, it is not without its risks. One of the most pressing concerns is privacy. Mental health data is deeply personal, and using AI raises questions about how this data is collected, stored, and shared. There have been instances where data breaches have exposed sensitive mental health information, causing significant harm to individuals.

Privacy Concerns and Data Security

The collection and analysis of personal data are central to AI's ability to provide personalised mental health care. However, this also makes the technology vulnerable to privacy breaches. For instance, AI systems that monitor individuals' mental health might collect data on their daily routines, social interactions, and even their private thoughts as recorded in journal entries. If this data were to be accessed by unauthorised parties, it could lead to significant privacy violations.

Moreover, even when data is anonymised, there is still a risk of re-identification, where anonymised data is matched with other datasets to reveal a person's identity. This is particularly concerning in the context of mental health, where the disclosure of sensitive information could lead to stigma, discrimination, or even job loss.

Bias in AI Systems

Another major concern is the potential for bias in AI algorithms. AI systems are only as good as the data on which they are trained. The AI's conclusions may also be biased if this data is biased—whether due to underrepresenting certain groups or flawed data collection methods. For example, an AI system trained primarily on data from white, middle-class individuals might not accurately diagnose mental health conditions in people from different racial, ethnic, or socioeconomic backgrounds.

This bias could lead to misdiagnoses or ineffective treatment recommendations, particularly for individuals from marginalised communities. For instance, studies have shown that certain demographic groups are less likely to be diagnosed with conditions like depression or anxiety, even when they exhibit similar symptoms to other groups. If AI systems are not carefully designed and tested to account for these biases, they could exacerbate existing health disparities.

Over-Reliance on AI and the Loss of Human Touch

Finally, there is the risk of over-reliance on AI. While AI can offer valuable support, it is not a substitute for human judgment and empathy. Mental health care is deeply personal, and the therapeutic relationship between patients and their therapist is often a key component of successful treatment. AI, for all its capabilities, cannot replicate the warmth, understanding, and trust that a human therapist can provide.

Moreover, there is a danger that as AI becomes more prevalent in mental health care, we might lose sight of the importance of human connection. For some individuals, interacting with an AI system might feel alienating or impersonal, potentially leading them to disengage from their treatment. It is essential to balance leveraging AI's capabilities and maintaining the human element of care.

Conclusion

AI has the potential to revolutionise mental health care, offering tools and insights that can significantly improve diagnosis, treatment, and prevention. However, it is essential to approach this technology with caution. Privacy concerns, potential biases, and the risk of over-reliance on AI are all serious issues that must be addressed. By maintaining a balanced view—embracing the benefits of AI while being mindful of its limitations—we can ensure that this powerful tool truly enhances mental health care for everyone.

As we progress, we must continue developing ethical guidelines and best practices for using AI in mental health care. This includes ensuring that AI systems are transparent, fair, and secure and used in ways that complement, rather than replace, the human touch. By doing so, we can harness the full potential of AI to improve mental health care while safeguarding the dignity and well-being of all individuals.

Trauma-Informed Care: Redefining Mental Health Support

Introduction

Trauma is an experience that fundamentally alters the way individuals perceive the world around them. For many, these experiences are deeply buried, influencing their thoughts, behaviours, and emotions in ways they might not fully understand. Trauma-Informed Care (TIC) is an approach that acknowledges the pervasive impact of trauma and seeks to provide mental health care that is sensitive to these experiences. This chapter explores the principles of TIC, its importance in modern mental health care, and how it is transforming the way we support those who have experienced trauma.

Understanding Trauma: A Hidden Influence

Trauma can result from a wide range of experiences — abuse, neglect, violence, loss, and natural disasters, to name a few. Trauma's subjective nature makes it complex; two people can experience the same event, but their psychological responses may differ. For some, trauma can lead to post-traumatic stress disorder (PTSD), while others may develop anxiety, depression, or other mental health conditions. Still, others may carry the scars of trauma without any diagnosable condition, yet their daily lives are still affected in significant ways.

The traditional approach to mental health care often focuses on treating symptoms without delving into the underlying causes. Trauma-Informed Care seeks to change that by shifting the focus from "What's wrong with you?" to "What happened to you?" This change in perspective is critical because it acknowledges that many mental health issues are rooted in past experiences, and understanding these experiences is vital to providing effective support.

The Complexity of Trauma

Trauma is not a one-size-fits-all experience. It can be acute, resulting from a single event like an accident or assault, or chronic, stemming from prolonged exposure to stressful events such as ongoing abuse or living in a war zone. There is also complex trauma, which involves exposure to multiple traumatic events, often of an invasive, interpersonal nature, occurring within specific contexts, such as childhood. Each type of trauma can have different effects on an individual's mental health, making it essential for care providers to recognise and respond to the nuances of each person's experience.

Moreover, trauma can have a ripple effect, impacting not only the individual but also their relationships, work, and community. For instance, a person who has experienced trauma may struggle with trust, making it difficult to form and maintain healthy relationships. In a work setting, they might have difficulty concentrating or managing stress, affecting their job performance. In broader terms, the cumulative effects of trauma on a community can manifest as increased rates of violence, substance abuse, and mental health disorders.

The Core Principles of Trauma-Informed Care

Trauma-Informed Care is built on a set of core principles designed to create a safe and supportive environment for individuals who have experienced trauma. These principles serve as the foundation for any trauma-informed approach and are crucial for fostering healing and resilience.

1. **Safety:** Ensuring the physical or psychological environment feels safe for the individual. This involves creating spaces where individuals feel secure and respected, both in the therapeutic setting and their broader environments, such as schools or workplaces. Safety also includes establishing clear boundaries and maintaining consistency to help individuals feel more in control of their experiences.

2. **Trustworthiness and Transparency:** Building and maintaining trust through open communication and consistency. This principle is particularly important for individuals who have experienced trauma, as they may have had their trust betrayed in the past. Transparency in providing care is essential to establish trust with those who

may be wary due to past traumas. This includes explaining the processes and goals of therapy or interventions clearly and being honest about potential challenges.

3. Peer Support: Recognising the value of shared experiences. Peer support is critical in Trauma-Informed Care, as individuals can connect with others who have faced similar challenges. Peer support groups or peer mentors who have navigated their trauma can offer invaluable insights and validation, helping others feel less isolated in their experiences.

4. Collaboration and Mutuality: Fostering a sense of partnership between the individual and the care provider. In Trauma-Informed Care, the provider and patient work together as equals, with the patient's voice central to the care process. This collaborative approach empowers individuals, making them active participants in their healing journey rather than passive recipients of care.

5. Empowerment, Voice, and Choice: Encouraging individuals to take an active role in their recovery. This principle focuses on empowering individuals to make choices about their care and ensuring they have a voice in their treatment. It involves recognising and building on the individual's strengths and encouraging autonomy, which can be particularly healing for those whose trauma involved a loss of control or agency.

6. Cultural, Historical, and Gender Issues: Acknowledging and addressing the various cultural, historical, and gender factors that influence how trauma is experienced and treated. This principle recognises that trauma does not occur in a vacuum and that individuals' cultural backgrounds, identities, and historical contexts can profoundly shape their experiences of trauma and healing. It is essential for care providers to be culturally competent and to tailor interventions in ways that are respectful and relevant to the individual's background.

Case Study: Healing Through Understanding

Consider the story of Sarah, a young woman in her early twenties who has been struggling with anxiety and depression since her teenage years. Traditional therapy had provided some relief, but it wasn't until she began working with a therapist trained in Trauma-Informed Care that she truly began to understand the roots of her struggles.

Through their work together, Sarah and her therapist uncovered that her anxiety was deeply connected to childhood experiences of emotional neglect and an unstable home environment. By acknowledging these past traumas and understanding how they influenced her current mental health, Sarah was able to make meaningful progress in her recovery. Her treatment plan was tailored to address these underlying issues, incorporating therapeutic techniques designed to build resilience and coping strategies specific to her needs.

For instance, her therapist employed techniques such as grounding exercises to help Sarah manage her anxiety when triggered by memories of her past. They also worked on developing a stronger sense of self-worth, challenging the negative beliefs about herself that had stemmed from her childhood experiences. Over time, Sarah noticed a significant reduction in her anxiety and depressive symptoms as she learned to process and integrate her past experiences more healthily.

Sarah's case illustrates how Trauma-Informed Care goes beyond symptom management, addressing the root causes of mental health issues and providing a more holistic approach to healing. By focusing on understanding and treating the underlying trauma, TIC can lead to more sustainable recovery and overall well-being.

The Impact of TIC on Schools and Communities

Trauma-Informed Care is not limited to one-on-one therapy sessions; it can also be implemented in schools, workplaces, and communities. Adopting TIC practices in these settings can create environments that promote healing and resilience on a broader scale.

Trauma-Informed Care in Schools

In schools, TIC can play a crucial role in helping educators understand the behavioural challenges that some students face as a result of trauma. Traditional disciplinary approaches, such as punishment or suspension, often fail to address the underlying issues that lead to disruptive behaviour. Instead, a trauma-informed approach seeks to understand what may trigger the behaviour and address the root causes.

For example, if a student acts out in class, a trauma-informed response might involve having a private conversation with the student to explore what is going on in their life. The educator might learn that the student is dealing with stress at home, such as a parent's illness or financial difficulties, which is affecting their ability to concentrate and behave in school. Rather than punishing the student, the educator can work with them to find solutions, such as offering extra support or connecting them with a school counsellor.

Moreover, schools that implement TIC practices often see improvements in the overall school climate, with reduced rates of suspension and expulsion, better academic outcomes, and a more positive environment for both students and staff. Training educators and staff in TIC principles is key to creating a school culture that supports all students, particularly those who have experienced trauma.

Trauma-Informed Care in Communities

Communities that adopt Trauma-Informed Care practices can create environments that promote healing and resilience. This might involve training law enforcement, healthcare providers, and community leaders to recognise and respond to trauma. For example, police officers trained in TIC might approach situations involving individuals in crisis with greater empathy and understanding, reducing the likelihood of escalation and increasing the chances of a peaceful resolution.

Healthcare providers who incorporate TIC into their practices are better equipped to recognise when a patient's physical health issues might be linked to unresolved trauma, leading to more comprehensive care. Community leaders can foster environments where trauma survivors feel supported and empowered through public health initiatives, support groups, or community events promoting mental health awareness.

By creating a culture of understanding and support, communities can help individuals feel safer and more empowered, ultimately leading to better mental health outcomes. TIC can also contribute to breaking cycles of trauma within communities, as individuals who receive appropriate care are less likely to perpetuate trauma in their own families and social circles.

The Future of Trauma-Informed Care

As the understanding of trauma and its impact on mental health continues to grow, Trauma-Informed Care is likely to become even more integral to mental health services. Future developments might include the integration of TIC with emerging technologies, such as AI, to provide more personalised and accessible care. For example, AI-driven tools could be used to identify trauma-related patterns in an individual's behaviour, offering tailored interventions that align with TIC principles.

Additionally, there is a growing recognition of the need for TIC in policy-making and organisational leadership. Organisations across sectors, including education, healthcare, criminal justice, and social services, are beginning to adopt TIC frameworks to improve outcomes and create more supportive environments for both staff and the people they serve.

Conclusion

Trauma-Informed Care (TIC) represents a significant shift in approaching mental health support. By recognising the profound and lasting impact of trauma and offering care that is sensitive to these experiences, TIC provides a more compassionate and effective framework for helping individuals heal and thrive. This approach challenges the traditional symptom-focused methods of mental health care, urging us to look deeper into the root causes of distress and dysfunction.

The principles of TIC—safety, trustworthiness, peer support, collaboration, empowerment, and cultural sensitivity—serve as a foundation for creating environments where individuals feel understood, respected, and capable of overcoming challenges. Whether applied in individual therapy, schools, or broader community settings, TIC has the potential to transform lives by addressing trauma's underlying effects and fostering resilience.

As the mental health field continues to evolve, integrating TIC with emerging technologies, such as AI, offers exciting possibilities for the future. These advancements could lead to even more personalised and accessible care, ensuring that trauma survivors receive the support they need to heal and build brighter futures.

Ultimately, Trauma-Informed Care is not just about treating mental health conditions — it's about recognising and honouring the human experience, acknowledging the pain that trauma causes, and providing a path toward healing that respects each individual's journey. By embracing TIC, we can move towards a mental health care system that truly supports all aspects of an individual's well-being, paving the way for a more compassionate and effective approach to mental health.

Building Trust in AI-Driven Mental Health Tools

Introduction

As AI-driven mental health tools become increasingly prevalent, the need for trust in these technologies becomes paramount. These tools offer unprecedented opportunities for personalised care and early intervention. Still, they also raise significant concerns about privacy, accuracy, and the potential loss of human connection in mental health care. Understanding how to navigate this new landscape is crucial, particularly for young adults and parents who may be using or considering these tools. This chapter explores the factors that influence trust in AI-driven mental health tools, the challenges that must be addressed, and how users can make informed decisions about the tools they choose.

The Importance of Trust in Mental Health Care

Trust is the cornerstone of any effective therapeutic relationship. In traditional mental health care, trust is built through personal interactions between the patient and the therapist. The therapist's empathy, reliability, and professionalism create a safe space for patients to share their thoughts and emotions, fostering a relationship based on mutual respect and understanding.

Trust must be established differently in the context of AI-driven mental health tools. These tools often operate without direct human interaction, requiring users to trust that the technology is reliable, accurate, and secure. This trust is not easily earned, especially when the technology is new and not fully understood by the general public. Building trust in AI involves ensuring users feel confident in the tool's ability to safeguard their personal information, provide accurate assessments, and effectively support their mental health journey.

Factors Influencing Trust in AI Tools

Several factors influence whether users trust AI-driven mental health tools:

1. Transparency: Transparency is fundamental in building trust. Users need to understand how the AI works, what data it collects, how that data is used, and who has access to it. Transparency involves clear communication from the developers and providers of these tools about the algorithms' functionality and limitations. For instance, if an AI tool analyses a user's social media activity to assess their mental state, users must be fully aware of this process and understand how their data is being utilised.

2. Privacy and Security: Given the sensitive nature of mental health data, privacy is a top concern. Users must trust that their information is securely stored, with robust encryption and strict access controls in place to prevent unauthorised access. Furthermore, users should be informed about how long their data will be retained and how it will be handled if they choose to discontinue using the tool. The recent increase in data breaches has heightened public awareness of these issues, making privacy and security essential components in building trust.

3. Accuracy: The effectiveness of AI tools depends on their ability to provide accurate assessments and recommendations. Users are likelier to trust AI tools validated through rigorous research and clinical testing. Accuracy is especially important in mental health care, where incorrect assessments can lead to inappropriate or harmful interventions. Developers must continuously refine their algorithms to improve accuracy and provide users with evidence of the tool's reliability and effectiveness.

4. Human Oversight: AI tools that include some level of human oversight—such as reviews by mental health professionals—are generally more trusted than those that operate entirely autonomously. Human oversight ensures that the AI's recommendations are interpreted correctly and applied in a way that is sensitive to the user's unique context. For example, an AI tool might flag certain behaviours indicative of depression. Still, a trained therapist can consider additional factors, such as the patient's life circumstances, before diagnosing or recommending treatment.

5. User Experience: A positive user experience can significantly enhance trust in AI-driven mental health tools. This includes ease of use, clear communication, and responsive support. Users are less likely to trust its recommendations if a tool is difficult to navigate or provides confusing feedback. On the other hand, a well-designed interface that is user-friendly and accessible can help users feel more comfortable and confident in using the tool regularly.

Case Study: Trusting AI in Crisis Situations

Consider the example of a mental health app that uses AI to monitor users' moods and provide real-time support. Emma, a 19-year-old university student, began using the app after struggling with anxiety and depression. The app offered daily check-ins, analysing her responses to gauge her mental state.

One evening, Emma was feeling particularly low. The app detected a significant drop in her mood and sent an alert recommending that she contact a counsellor immediately. The alert also provided resources for crisis hotlines and local mental health services. Although initially hesitant, Emma decided to follow the app's advice and contacted a counsellor, who helped her through the crisis.

This situation highlights the importance of trust in AI-driven tools. Emma trusted the app because it consistently provided her with helpful insights and demonstrated a commitment to her privacy and well-being. This trust was not built overnight; it developed over time as the app proved its reliability and accuracy. Because Emma trusted the app to assess her mental state and provide reliable advice accurately, she was able to get the help she needed during a critical moment.

Challenges in Building Trust

Despite the potential benefits, several challenges must be addressed to build and maintain trust in AI-driven mental health tools:

Data Privacy Concerns: High-profile data breaches have made many people wary of sharing personal information online. AI tools must demonstrate that they can protect user data from unauthorised access. This includes implementing strong encryption, regular security audits, and transparent privacy policies outlining how user data is handled and protected. Additionally, developers should consider offering users the ability to control their data, such as by opting out of certain data collection practices or deleting their data entirely.

Algorithmic Bias: If the data used to train AI tools is biased, the tools themselves may produce biased outcomes. This is particularly concerning in mental health, where biased assessments could lead to inappropriate or ineffective treatment recommendations. For example, an AI tool that is trained primarily on data from a specific demographic group may not accurately assess individuals from other backgrounds, leading to misdiagnoses or suboptimal treatment. Addressing algorithmic bias requires careful consideration of the training data used and ongoing testing and refinement of the algorithms to ensure they are fair and inclusive.

Lack of Human Interaction: Some users may find it difficult to trust a tool that lacks the human touch. For these individuals, AI-driven tools might feel impersonal or even alienating. Human interaction is critical to mental health care, allowing for empathy, understanding, and personalised support. To address this challenge, developers could consider integrating AI tools with human backing, such as offering access to mental health professionals who can provide guidance and context for the AI's recommendations.

Regulation and Standards: The AI mental health field is still relatively new, and few established standards or regulations exist. Without these, users may have difficulty discerning which tools are trustworthy. Establishing industry-wide standards and regulations for AI-driven mental health tools is essential to ensure consistency, safety, and efficacy. This might include guidelines for data privacy, accuracy, and ethical use of AI and certification processes to verify that tools meet these standards.

Conclusion

Building trust in AI-driven mental health tools is a complex but essential task. As these tools become more integrated into our mental health care systems, it is crucial to ensure that they are transparent, secure, accurate, and user-friendly. By addressing the challenges and focusing on the factors that enhance trust, we can create a future where AI tools are valuable allies in improving mental health.

Trust is not built overnight, nor is it guaranteed. It must be earned through consistent performance, transparency, and a commitment to safeguarding the user's well-being. As developers and providers of AI-driven mental health tools, it is our responsibility to prioritise the user's trust, ensuring that these tools meet and exceed expectations. By doing so, we can harness the full potential of AI to enhance mental health care, providing support that is both innovative and deeply rooted in the principles of trust, empathy, and respect.

Setting Boundaries: The Digital Detox Movement

Introduction

Social media has become central to our daily lives in today's hyperconnected world. From staying in touch with friends to consuming news and entertainment, platforms like Instagram, Twitter, and TikTok have become indispensable tools. However, this constant connectivity comes with a price. Excessive social media use has been linked to a range of mental health issues, including anxiety, depression, and poor sleep quality. For young adults and parents alike, understanding how to set healthy boundaries with social media is crucial for maintaining mental well-being. This chapter explores the digital detox movement, its benefits, and practical strategies for reclaiming control over our digital lives.

The Impact of Social Media on Mental Health

The effects of social media on mental health are well-documented and multifaceted. Numerous studies have shown that heavy social media use can lead to increased feelings of loneliness, anxiety, and depression. This is particularly true for young people, who often face the pressures of maintaining a curated online presence. The comparison culture fostered by platforms like Instagram, where users are constantly exposed to images of seemingly perfect lives, can exacerbate feelings of inadequacy and low self-esteem. The constant comparison to others' highlight reels can lead to a distorted perception of reality, where one's life seems less exciting or fulfilling.

Social media also significantly impacts sleep patterns, with many users finding themselves scrolling through their feeds late into the night. The blue light emitted by screens interferes with melatonin production, the hormone responsible for regulating sleep, leading to insomnia and other sleep disorders. Over time, poor sleep can contribute to a host of mental health problems, including depression, anxiety, and cognitive impairments. Additionally, the habit of staying up late to check social media can disrupt the body's natural circadian rhythm, making it difficult to achieve restorative sleep.

Beyond the psychological effects, social media can also affect physical health. Prolonged screen time is associated with sedentary behaviour, which can lead to physical health issues such as obesity, cardiovascular problems, and musculoskeletal disorders. The combination of these physical and mental health challenges underscores the need for a balanced approach to social media use.

The Rise of the Digital Detox Movement

In response to these concerns, the digital detox movement has gained significant momentum in recent years. A digital detox involves taking a break from electronic devices, particularly social media, to reduce stress and improve mental health. For some, this might mean setting aside specific times of the day to be offline, while for others, it could involve longer breaks or even quitting social media altogether.

The idea behind a digital detox is simple: by disconnecting from the constant barrage of online information, individuals can reduce stress, improve focus, and reconnect with the world around them. This movement has been supported by mental health professionals who advocate for a more mindful approach to technology use. The digital detox is not just about reducing screen time; it is about re-engaging with real-life experiences, fostering deeper connections with others, and finding joy in activities that do not involve screens.

The Psychological Benefits of a Digital Detox

A digital detox can lead to numerous psychological benefits. By stepping away from the pressures of social media, individuals may experience a reduction in anxiety and an improvement in mood. The absence of constant notifications and the temptation to check for updates can lead to a calmer, more focused mind. Moreover, without the pressure to document and share every moment online, individuals may find themselves more present in their daily lives, leading to a greater sense of satisfaction and fulfilment.

Additionally, a break from social media can help individuals reconnect with their personal interests and hobbies. Whether reading, painting, hiking, or spending time with loved ones, these offline activities can provide a sense of accomplishment and joy often diminished by the endless scroll of social media. For many, a digital detox is an opportunity to rediscover the simple pleasures of life that are often overshadowed by the digital world.

Practical Strategies for Setting Social Media Boundaries

Setting boundaries with social media doesn't necessarily mean giving it up entirely. Instead, it's about finding a balance that works for you. Here are some practical strategies for managing social media use:

1. Set Time Limits: Many smartphones now offer screen time tracking features that allow you to set daily limits for app usage. Use these tools to monitor your time on social media and set goals for reducing it. For instance, you might start by limiting social media use to 30 minutes a day and gradually reducing that time as you become more comfortable with being offline.

2. Designate Tech-Free Zones: Establish certain areas of your home as tech-free zones, such as the dining room or bedroom. This can help create a physical boundary between you and your devices, making it easier to disconnect. For example, keeping your bedroom free of screens can create a more restful environment that promotes better sleep.

3. Schedule Regular Breaks: Consider taking regular breaks from social media, whether for a few hours or a full day each week. Use this time to engage in offline activities that bring you joy, such as reading, exercising, or spending time with loved ones. Regular breaks can help reset your relationship with social media, making it a tool that enhances your life rather than dominates it.

4. Curate Your Feed: Take control of your social media experience by unfollowing accounts that make you anxious or insecure. Instead, follow accounts that inspire and uplift you, creating a more positive online environment. Curating your feed to include content that aligns with your values and interests can make social media a more enjoyable and enriching experience.

5. Mindful Consumption: Practice mindfulness when using social media. Before you open an app, ask yourself why you're doing it and how it makes you feel. If you find that social media is causing you stress, it might be time to take a step back. Mindful consumption encourages you to use social media intentionally rather than as a mindless habit, which can reduce its negative impact on your mental health.

Case Study: The Benefits of a Digital Detox

Consider the case of Samantha, a 22-year-old college student who became increasingly overwhelmed by social media. Between keeping up with friends, managing her online persona, and the constant stream of news, she felt anxious and stressed. After learning about the digital detox movement, she decided to take a week-long break from social media.

During this time, Samantha focused on her hobbies, spent more time outdoors, and reconnected with friends. She also practised mindfulness and meditation, which helped her manage the stress that her online activities had previously exacerbated. By the end of the week, Samantha noticed a significant improvement in her mood and mental clarity. She felt less anxious and more present in her daily life. After her detox, Samantha returned to social media with new boundaries. She now limits her use to 30 minutes a day and regularly takes breaks to maintain her mental health.

Samantha's experience illustrates a digital detox's profound impact on mental well-being. By stepping away from the pressures of social media, she regained control of her mental health, improved her focus, and enjoyed a greater sense of balance in her life.

The Long-Term Benefits of Digital Detoxing

While a short-term digital detox can offer immediate benefits, incorporating regular digital detoxes into your routine can lead to long-term improvements in mental health. Over time, individuals who regularly disconnect from social media may experience sustained reductions in anxiety and depression, improved sleep quality, and a deeper sense of contentment. The habit of taking regular breaks from the digital world can also foster a healthier relationship with technology, where it serves as a tool for enhancing life rather than a source of stress.

Moreover, setting boundaries with social media can empower individuals to be more intentional with their time and energy. Instead of being reactive to the constant demands of the digital world, they can proactively choose how to spend their time, leading to greater productivity, creativity, and overall life satisfaction.

Conclusion

The digital detox movement offers a powerful antidote to the mental health challenges posed by excessive social media use. Individuals can reduce stress, improve focus, and reclaim control over their digital lives by setting healthy boundaries and taking regular breaks. For young adults and parents, understanding the importance of these boundaries is crucial for maintaining mental well-being in a connected world.

As we continue to navigate the digital age, it is essential to remember that while social media can be a valuable tool, it is also important to protect our mental health by setting limits and practising mindful consumption. By doing so, we can enjoy the benefits of technology without sacrificing our well-being.

Virtual Reality in Psychiatric Care: The Future of Treatment

Introduction

Virtual Reality (VR) has long been associated with gaming and entertainment, but its potential extends beyond these realms. In recent years, VR has emerged as a powerful tool in psychiatric care, offering new ways to treat conditions such as anxiety, post-traumatic stress disorder (PTSD), and phobias. For young adults and parents navigating the world of mental health, understanding how VR is being used in therapy can open up new avenues for treatment. This chapter explores the rise of VR in psychiatric care, the science behind it, and how it is revolutionising mental health treatment.

The Science of VR Therapy

Virtual Reality therapy involves using VR technology to create simulated environments that patients can interact with in a controlled setting. These environments are designed to evoke specific emotional responses, allowing therapists to guide patients through therapeutic exercises that would be difficult or impossible to replicate in the real world.

How VR Works in Therapy

In a typical VR therapy session, a patient wears a VR headset that immerses them in a three-dimensional environment. This environment can be customised to suit the specific therapeutic needs of the patient. For instance, if a patient is being treated for fear of heights, the VR environment might simulate standing on a high ledge or crossing a narrow bridge. The therapist can control the environment, gradually increasing exposure to the feared situation in a manageable way for the patient.

The immersive nature of VR makes it an incredibly effective tool for this type of therapy. Patients are fully engaged in the virtual environment, which can help them process their emotions and learn new coping strategies. The sense of presence that VR creates—that is, the feeling of being physically present in a non-physical world—can make the therapeutic experience more impactful than traditional methods.

Applications of VR in Mental Health

One of the most well-known applications of VR in mental health is exposure therapy. This form of treatment is often used to treat anxiety disorders, PTSD, and phobias by gradually exposing patients to the objects or situations that trigger their fear in a safe and controlled environment. For example, a person with a fear of flying might use VR to experience a simulated flight, allowing them to confront their fear without the risks associated with real-world exposure. This controlled exposure helps the patient gradually desensitise to the fear-inducing stimulus, reducing their anxiety over time.

Another promising application of VR is in the treatment of PTSD, particularly in veterans. VR allows these individuals to confront traumatic memories in a controlled and supportive environment. By revisiting these memories in a virtual setting, patients can work through their trauma with the guidance of a therapist, who can help them reprocess these experiences and develop healthier responses.

VR is also being explored as a cognitive behavioural therapy (CBT) tool, where patients can practice real-life scenarios in a safe environment. For example, someone with social anxiety might use VR to simulate a public speaking event, allowing them to practice coping strategies and build confidence before facing such situations in real life.

Case Study: VR and PTSD

Consider the case of Alex, a 25-year-old veteran who has been struggling with PTSD since returning from deployment. Traditional therapy provided some relief, but Alex found it difficult to fully engage in the process, particularly when it came to discussing traumatic memories.

His therapist suggested trying VR therapy as part of his treatment plan. Using VR, Alex was able to revisit simulated versions of the environments that triggered his PTSD but in a safe and controlled way. The therapist guided Alex through these sessions, helping him process his emotions and develop healthier responses to his triggers.

Over time, Alex noticed a significant reduction in his PTSD symptoms. He felt more in control of his emotions and better equipped to handle situations that had previously triggered intense anxiety. For Alex, VR therapy provided a way to confront and heal from his trauma in a way that traditional therapy had not been able to achieve.

Alex's case illustrates how VR can be a transformative tool in treating PTSD. By providing a safe space to confront and process traumatic memories, VR can help individuals like Alex regain control over their lives and reduce the impact of their trauma on daily functioning.

Advantages of VR in Mental Health Treatment

The use of VR in psychiatric care offers several advantages over traditional therapeutic methods:

1. Controlled Environment: VR allows therapists to create highly controlled environments that can be tailored to the needs of each patient. This level of control is difficult to achieve in the real world, making VR an invaluable tool for exposure therapy. For example, a therapist can adjust the intensity of the virtual experience based on the patient's comfort level, ensuring that the exposure is gradual and manageable.

2. Safe Exploration of Emotions: VR provides a safe space for patients dealing with trauma or intense phobias to explore and process difficult emotions. The virtual nature of the experience allows patients to confront their fears without the risk of real-world harm. This is particularly beneficial for individuals who might find it too overwhelming to face their fears in reality but are willing to engage with them in a virtual setting.

3. Accessibility: As VR technology becomes more affordable and accessible, it has the potential to reach a wider audience. This could make effective mental health treatment available to those who might not otherwise have access to it, particularly in remote or underserved areas. For example, a person living in a rural area with limited access to mental health professionals could use VR therapy to receive treatment from a specialist located elsewhere.

4. Engagement: The immersive nature of VR can increase patient engagement in therapy. For young adults, who are often more comfortable with technology, VR may make therapy feel more relevant and accessible. VR's interactive and immersive aspects can make therapy sessions more engaging, helping patients stay motivated and committed to their treatment.

5. Customisation: VR therapy can be tailored to each patient's individual needs. Therapists can adjust the virtual environments to suit the specific triggers and challenges of the patient, making the therapy more effective. This level of customisation is difficult to achieve in traditional therapy settings.

Challenges and Considerations

Despite its potential, the use of VR in psychiatric care is not without challenges. One of the primary concerns is the cost of the technology. While VR headsets have become more affordable, they still represent a significant investment, particularly for smaller practices or individual therapists. The initial cost of the equipment, along with the need for specialised software and training, can be a barrier to widespread adoption.

Additionally, there are concerns about the potential for VR to cause discomfort or exacerbate symptoms in some patients. Motion sickness, for example, is a common side effect of VR use, and for individuals with certain mental health conditions, the immersive nature of VR could potentially trigger adverse reactions. It is essential for therapists to carefully assess the suitability of VR for each patient and monitor their responses during sessions.

There is also the question of how VR therapy fits into the broader landscape of mental health care. While VR can be a powerful tool, it is not a one-size-fits-all solution. It is most effective as part of a comprehensive treatment plan that includes traditional therapy and other interventions. For instance, VR might be used in conjunction with CBT, medication, or other therapeutic approaches to provide a holistic treatment plan.

Ethical Considerations in VR Therapy

As with any new technology, the use of VR in mental health treatment raises important ethical considerations. One concern is the potential for VR to be overused or misused, particularly if it is seen as a "quick fix" for complex mental health issues. Therapists and patients must ensure that VR is used appropriately and ethically, clearly understanding its limitations and potential risks.

Another ethical concern is the need for informed consent. Before agreeing to participate, patients must fully understand what VR therapy involves, including the potential risks and benefits. This includes being informed about the immersive nature of the experience and the possibility of experiencing discomfort or adverse reactions.

Conclusion

Virtual Reality is revolutionising the field of psychiatric care, offering new ways to treat a range of mental health conditions. VR can help patients confront and overcome their fears safely and effectively by providing a controlled, immersive environment for therapeutic exercises. However, it is essential to approach this technology with an understanding of its limitations and to use it as part of a broader treatment strategy. For young adults and parents, understanding the potential and challenges of VR therapy can help them make informed decisions about whether it might be a suitable option in their mental health journey.

As VR technology continues to evolve, it will likely play an increasingly important role in mental health care. However, it is crucial to balance innovation with caution, ensuring that VR is used in ways that enhance, rather than replace, traditional therapeutic approaches. By doing so, we can harness the full potential of VR to improve mental health outcomes while maintaining the human connection at the heart of effective therapy.

The Integration of Trauma-Informed Care into AI Technologies

Introduction

In the evolving landscape of mental health care, the convergence of Trauma-Informed Care (TIC) and Artificial Intelligence (AI) represents a promising frontier. Trauma-Informed Care, which focuses on understanding and addressing the impact of trauma with compassion and sensitivity, has proven to be an effective approach in various therapeutic settings. When combined with AI, TIC has the potential to reach more people, offer more personalised support, and improve mental health outcomes on a broader scale. This chapter explores how AI technologies are being integrated with Trauma-Informed Care principles to create innovative solutions in mental health care.

The Synergy of AI and Trauma-Informed Care

AI technologies are designed to process vast amounts of data and identify patterns that human practitioners might miss. In the context of Trauma-Informed Care, AI can recognise subtle indicators of trauma in a person's behaviour, speech patterns, or physiological responses. By analysing these indicators, AI can help mental health professionals develop more personalised and effective treatment plans aligned with TIC principles.

Personalisation and Early Intervention

One of the most significant advantages of integrating AI with Trauma-Informed Care is the ability to personalise interventions and provide early support. AI can monitor various data sources, including wearable devices, social media activity, and communication patterns, to detect signs of distress that might otherwise go unnoticed. For example, a slight change in sleep patterns, increased heart rate, or a shift in the tone of voice can all be indicators of underlying trauma. AI systems can process these subtle cues in real-time, alerting both the individual and their therapist to potential issues before they escalate.

This ability to intervene early is particularly valuable in trauma-related care, where timely support can prevent the worsening of symptoms and contribute to more effective recovery. By offering personalised recommendations based on real-time data, AI systems can help individuals manage their mental health more proactively, reducing the likelihood of severe episodes or crises.

AI-Powered Support Tools

AI-powered chatbots and virtual assistants are at the forefront of this integration. These tools can be trained to recognise signs of distress or trauma in users' communications, offering immediate support in the form of coping strategies, mindfulness exercises, or connections to mental health resources. The key to these tools' effectiveness is their design within the framework of Trauma-Informed Care, ensuring that they respond in ways that are empathetic, non-judgmental, and supportive.

For example, an AI chatbot might engage a user in a conversation about their day. If the user's responses indicate heightened anxiety or distress, the chatbot could offer calming techniques or suggest contacting a therapist. The AI's ability to recognise and respond to these cues in real-time provides continuous support, especially during moments when human help might not be immediately available.

Case Study: AI and TIC in Action

Consider the case of Noah, a teenager who had experienced bullying at school, leading to significant anxiety and depression. Noah began using a mental health app that integrated AI with Trauma-Informed Care principles. The app used AI to monitor Noah's daily journal entries, social media activity, and biometric data from his wearable device.

Over time, the AI detected patterns that suggested Noah was struggling with the aftereffects of his traumatic experiences. The app responded by offering Noah personalised coping strategies, such as breathing exercises and mindfulness activities, designed to help him manage his anxiety in the moment. The app also alerted Noah's therapist, who was able to adjust his treatment plan to address his underlying trauma better.

Through the combination of AI and TIC, Noah received continuous, personalised support that was sensitive to his trauma history. This approach helped Noah manage his symptoms more effectively and empowered him to take an active role in his recovery. The use of AI allowed for more precise tracking of Noah's progress, enabling his therapist to make data-driven decisions about his care.

Challenges and Considerations

While the integration of AI and Trauma-Informed Care offers significant potential, it also presents several challenges that must be carefully managed.

Data Diversity and Bias

One of the primary concerns is ensuring that AI technologies are trained on diverse and representative data sets. Suppose the data used to train AI systems is not diverse. In that case, the AI may fail to recognise trauma-related patterns in individuals from different cultural or socioeconomic backgrounds, leading to biased or ineffective interventions. For example, an AI system trained primarily on data from a specific demographic may not accurately interpret the signs of trauma in someone from a different cultural background, resulting in inappropriate recommendations.

Addressing this challenge requires a commitment to using inclusive data sets that reflect the diversity of the populations served. This includes considering factors such as race, gender, age, and cultural background when developing and training AI systems. Moreover, continuous monitoring and updating of AI algorithms are necessary to ensure they remain accurate and relevant as more data becomes available.

Privacy and Data Security

The reliance on AI in trauma-informed interventions raises ethical questions about privacy and data security. Given the sensitive nature of trauma-related information, AI systems must be designed with robust safeguards to protect users' data and privacy. This includes implementing strong encryption, secure data storage, and clear policies about how data is used and shared.

Users must also be informed about the data collection process and given the option to control their data. Transparency is key to building trust in AI-driven tools, particularly when dealing with vulnerable populations. It is essential that users feel confident that their personal information is being handled with the utmost care and that they have control over who can access it.

Maintaining the Human Element

Another challenge is ensuring that AI tools do not replace the human element of care. While AI can provide valuable support, it cannot replicate a trained therapist's empathy and understanding of the therapeutic relationship. The human connection in trauma-informed care is crucial, as it fosters trust and allows for deeper emotional healing. As such, AI should be viewed as a supplement to, rather than a replacement for, human-led trauma-informed care.

Integrating AI into mental health care should enhance the therapeutic process by providing additional tools and insights that therapists can use to support their patients better. For example, AI can help therapists monitor their patients' progress between sessions, identify areas where additional support might be needed, and personalise treatment plans. However, the final decisions about care should always involve human judgement and compassion.

The Future of AI-Driven Trauma-Informed Care

Integrating AI and Trauma-Informed Care will likely become increasingly sophisticated as technology advances. Developments in natural language processing, machine learning, and biometric monitoring will enable AI systems to understand better and respond to the nuances of trauma. These advancements could lead to developing even more personalised and effective mental health interventions.

For instance, future AI systems might be able to detect more complex patterns of trauma-related behaviour by analysing a broader range of data sources, such as facial expressions, body language, and physiological responses. These systems could provide real-time feedback to therapists, helping them adjust their approaches on the fly to meet the needs of their patients better.

However, it will be essential to continue developing these technologies within the framework of Trauma-Informed Care, ensuring that they remain compassionate, non-judgmental, and supportive of the user's well-being. Ethical oversight will be crucial to prevent potential misuse of AI in mental health care, such as over-reliance on automated systems or the erosion of personal privacy.

Conclusion

Integrating Trauma-Informed Care into AI technologies represents a powerful opportunity to enhance mental health care. By combining AI insights with the compassion and sensitivity of TIC, we can create tools that are effective and deeply respectful of the individual's lived experience. As these technologies continue to evolve, they hold the promise of improving mental health outcomes for countless individuals who have experienced trauma.

The future of AI-driven Trauma-Informed Care lies in its ability to balance technological innovation with human empathy. By maintaining this balance, we can ensure that AI serves as a valuable ally in the ongoing effort to support and heal those affected by trauma. AI's careful and ethical integration into TIC can revolutionise mental health care, making it more accessible, personalised, and effective for all.

Measuring Success: The Future of AI in Mental Health

Introduction

As Artificial Intelligence (AI) becomes more deeply integrated into mental health care, the question of how to measure its success is increasingly important. Unlike traditional therapies, where outcomes are often measured through direct patient feedback and clinical assessments, AI-driven mental health tools present new challenges and opportunities for evaluation. This chapter delves into the future of AI in mental health, focusing on how success can be measured, the importance of continuous improvement, and what this means for mental health care.

Defining Success in AI-Driven Mental Health Care

Success in AI-driven mental health care can be measured in several ways. The most straightforward measure is the improvement in patient outcomes. This includes reductions in symptoms such as anxiety, depression, and PTSD, as well as improvements in overall well-being and quality of life. For instance, AI systems might track how a patient's mood or anxiety levels change over time, using this data to assess the effectiveness of specific interventions.

Another critical aspect of measuring success in AI-driven care is the system's ability to provide timely and accurate interventions that prevent mental health crises before they escalate. For example, if an AI tool can predict when a patient will likely experience a significant depressive episode and prompt early intervention, this can be considered a considerable success.

However, success in AI-driven care goes beyond just clinical outcomes. It also includes factors like user engagement, satisfaction, and adherence to treatment plans. AI tools that are easy to use, intuitive, and provide clear value to the user are more likely to be successful in the long term. For instance, an AI app that consistently receives positive feedback from users for its ease of use and helpfulness in managing symptoms is more likely to sustain engagement and achieve better outcomes. Additionally, AI must be evaluated on its ability to adapt and learn over time, improving its accuracy and effectiveness as it processes more data.

The Role of Data in Measuring Success

One of AI's unique advantages in mental health care is its ability to collect and analyse large amounts of data. This data can provide valuable insights into the AI's performance and where improvements might be needed. For example, AI can track patterns in user behaviour, such as how often they use the app, which features they engage with, and how their mental health metrics change over time.

This data-driven approach enables continuous improvement, as developers can refine algorithms based on real-world usage and outcomes. For instance, if data shows that users who engage with a particular app feature tend to have better outcomes, developers can enhance that feature and encourage more users to take advantage of it. Conversely, if a feature is underused or associated with poor outcomes, it may be revised or removed.

Moreover, data-driven insights can help refine treatment plans, making them more personalised and responsive to the individual's needs. For example, suppose an AI system notices that a user's anxiety levels spike at specific times of day or in response to particular activities. In that case, it can tailor its recommendations to address these triggers more effectively.

Case Study: Measuring Success in an AI-Driven Mental Health App

Consider the case of an AI-driven mental health app designed to help users manage stress and anxiety. The app uses machine learning algorithms to provide personalised recommendations based on the user's daily inputs, such as mood, sleep patterns, and activity levels. Over time, the app tracks the user's progress and adjusts its recommendations accordingly.

To measure the success of this app, developers look at several key metrics. First, they monitor clinical outcomes, such as reductions in reported anxiety levels and improvements in sleep quality. For example, if users report a significant decrease in anxiety after consistently following the app's recommendations, this would be considered a successful outcome.

They also track user engagement, noting how often users interact with the app and which features are most popular. High levels of engagement suggest that users find the app helpful and are likely to continue using it, which is essential for long-term success. For instance, an app feature that provides quick mindfulness exercises might be particularly popular and, therefore, a key focus for further development.

Additionally, developers collect user feedback to gauge satisfaction and identify areas for improvement. This feedback is critical for ensuring that the app meets its users' needs and remains effective in the long term. By combining clinical data with user feedback, developers can create a comprehensive picture of the app's success and areas for further development.

Challenges in Measuring AI Success

Measuring the success of AI in mental health care is not without its challenges. One of the primary concerns is ensuring that the data used to evaluate AI is accurate and representative. If the data is biased or incomplete, it can lead to skewed results that do not accurately reflect the AI's performance. For example, suppose an AI system is primarily trained on data from a specific demographic group. In that case, it may not perform as well for users from different backgrounds, leading to misleading conclusions about its effectiveness.

Another challenge is the potential for over-reliance on quantitative data. While metrics like symptom reduction and user engagement are important, they do not capture the full complexity of mental health care. Qualitative measures, such as user experiences and the therapeutic relationship, are also critical for understanding the true impact of AI-driven interventions. For instance, while an AI tool might show high engagement rates, it is also essential to assess whether users feel supported and understood by the tool, as these factors significantly influence mental health outcomes.

Moreover, there is the issue of long-term effectiveness. AI tools may show promising results in the short term, but it is essential to monitor their performance over time to ensure they continue to be effective. This requires ongoing evaluation and a commitment to continuous improvement. For instance, an AI tool that helps users manage anxiety effectively in the first few months of use might lose its effectiveness if it does not evolve with the user's changing needs or if new stressors emerge.

The Future of AI in Mental Health: Continuous Improvement

As AI technologies evolve, the focus will increasingly shift towards continuous improvement. This means refining algorithms, improving data analysis, and ensuring AI tools respond to users' changing needs. Developers must be committed to ongoing research, user feedback, and clinical testing to ensure that AI tools continue to deliver high-quality care.

In the future, we may see AI tools that are even more personalised, adaptive, and intuitive, offering mental health care tailored to the individual. For example, future AI systems might integrate more advanced biometric data, such as heart rate variability and cortisol levels, to provide even more accurate and timely interventions. These systems could also become more adept at understanding and responding to the context of the user's experiences, such as recognising when a user is in a high-stress environment and adjusting recommendations accordingly.

However, achieving this level of sophistication will require measuring success comprehensively, considering both quantitative and qualitative factors. For instance, developers might need to balance the need for data-driven insights with the importance of maintaining a human-centred approach that values empathy and understanding.

Ethical Considerations in Measuring AI Success

As AI plays a more prominent role in mental health care, ethical considerations around measuring success will become increasingly important. One key concern is ensuring that AI tools do not perpetuate existing biases in mental health care. For example, if an AI system is more effective for certain demographic groups than others, this could exacerbate health disparities rather than reduce them.

It is also essential to ensure that AI-driven interventions respect users' autonomy and privacy. This includes being transparent about how data is collected and used and ensuring that users have control over their data. Moreover, as AI tools become more integrated into mental health care, there will be a need to establish clear guidelines and standards for evaluating their success, ensuring that these tools are used responsibly and ethically.

Conclusion

Measuring AI's success in mental health care is complex but essential. By focusing on clinical outcomes, user engagement, and continuous improvement, we can ensure that AI-driven tools are genuinely effective in improving mental health outcomes. As these technologies continue to develop, they have the potential to revolutionise mental health care, offering more personalised, responsive, and effective interventions for those in need.

The future of AI in mental health care lies in its ability to combine the precision of data-driven insights with compassion and empathy, which are central to effective therapy. By measuring success in a way that reflects both these aspects, we can create AI tools that deliver results and support the overall well-being of those who use them.

Ethical Considerations and the Future of Mental Health Technology

Introduction

As mental health care increasingly integrates advanced technologies such as Artificial Intelligence (AI), Virtual Reality (VR), and data analytics, a new set of ethical considerations comes to the forefront. These technologies have the potential to revolutionise mental health care, making it more personalised, accessible, and effective. However, they also raise significant ethical questions that must be addressed to ensure that these advancements benefit everyone. This chapter explores the moral issues surrounding mental health technology, including privacy, data security, algorithmic bias, and the importance of maintaining the human element in care.

The Challenge of Privacy in the Digital Age

One of the most pressing ethical concerns in mental health technology is privacy. Mental health data is some of the most sensitive information a person can share, encompassing personal thoughts, emotions, and behaviours. As AI-driven tools and apps collect and analyse this data, ensuring its protection becomes paramount.

Data Privacy Risks and Safeguards

Despite advancements in data encryption and cybersecurity, the risk of data breaches remains a significant concern. High-profile breaches in other sectors, such as finance and healthcare, have shown that no system is foolproof. In the context of mental health, a breach could expose intimate details of a person's life, leading to stigma, discrimination, or even legal repercussions. For instance, sensitive information about a person's mental health condition being exposed could impact their employment opportunities, relationships, or social standing.

Moreover, there is the question of data ownership. Who owns the data when users share it with mental health apps or platforms? In many cases, the terms of service grant the company significant rights over the data, including using it for research or even selling it to third parties. This raises ethical questions about consent and whether users fully understand what they agree to when using these technologies. Users often skip reading lengthy privacy policies, potentially unaware of how their data might be used beyond the app's primary purpose.

The Role of Informed Consent

Informed consent is another critical aspect of data privacy. Users must be fully informed about what data is being collected, how it will be used, who will have access to it, and the potential risks involved. This information should be communicated in clear, accessible language, avoiding the legal jargon that often obscures the true nature of the agreement. Ethical mental health technologies should prioritise transparency, giving users control over their data and ensuring their consent is obtained freely and without coercion.

Algorithmic Bias and Fairness

Another critical ethical issue is algorithmic bias. AI systems are only as good as the data they are trained on. If the training data underrepresents certain groups or reflects historical inequalities, the AI's outputs will also be biased. This can lead to inaccurate diagnoses, inappropriate treatment recommendations, or the exclusion of specific populations from the benefits of AI-driven mental health care.

Examples of Algorithmic Bias

For example, suppose an AI system is trained primarily on data from middle-class white individuals. In that case, it may perform poorly for people of colour, individuals from lower socioeconomic backgrounds, or those with different cultural experiences. The result could be a system that fails to recognise the symptoms of mental health conditions in these groups or that provides less effective treatment recommendations. This could exacerbate existing disparities in mental health care rather than reduce them, particularly if these AI systems are widely adopted without addressing these biases.

Mitigating Bias in AI Systems

Addressing these issues requires a multi-faceted approach. Ensuring that AI systems are trained on diverse and representative data sets is essential. This means actively seeking out and including data from underrepresented groups to create algorithms that can accurately serve a broader range of people. Additionally, ongoing auditing and transparency are needed to identify and mitigate emerging biases. Regular assessments of AI systems should be conducted to ensure that they remain fair and effective over time.

Developers should also consider involving ethicists, sociologists, and representatives from diverse communities in AI development's design and testing phases. This collaborative approach can help identify potential biases early on and ensure that the final product is as equitable as possible.

Maintaining the Human Element in Mental Health Care

While technology can enhance mental health care in many ways, it is crucial not to lose sight of the importance of human interaction in the therapeutic process. Empathy, trust, and the therapeutic alliance between patients and their providers are foundational elements of adequate mental health care. These elements are difficult, if not impossible, to replicate with technology alone.

The Limitations of Technology in Therapy

As AI and other technologies become more prevalent, the human element of care could be diminished. For instance, chatbots and virtual therapists can provide 24/7 support but lack the depth of understanding and empathy that a trained human therapist can offer. While these tools can be valuable supplements, they should not replace human care, especially for those with complex or severe mental health conditions. The nuances of human emotions, the need for tailored responses, and the ability to understand context are areas where technology still falls short compared to human therapists.

Case Study: Balancing Technology and Human Care

Consider the case of Maria, a young adult who has been struggling with anxiety and depression. She uses a popular mental health app that employs AI to provide daily check-ins, mood tracking, and personalised coping strategies. The app has helped manage her symptoms, but Maria feels something is missing.

Maria decides to seek a therapist to supplement her app use. Through therapy, she can explore deeper issues that the app couldn't address, such as unresolved trauma and relationship difficulties. The combination of AI-driven support and traditional therapy provides Maria with a comprehensive approach to her mental health, highlighting the importance of maintaining the human element in care.

Maria's experience underscores the need for a balanced approach where technology enhances rather than replaces the human aspects of mental health care. This balance allows for the benefits of AI, such as accessibility and personalisation, while preserving the essential human connection that underpins successful therapeutic outcomes.

The Role of Regulation and Standards

As mental health technologies continue to evolve, there is a growing need for regulation and standards to ensure these tools are safe, effective, and ethical. Currently, regulating mental health apps and AI-driven tools is inconsistent, with many products on the market lacking rigorous testing or oversight.

Establishing Standards for Mental Health Technology

Establishing clear standards for developing, testing, and deploying mental health technologies is essential for protecting consumers and ensuring that these tools deliver on their promises. This could involve government regulation, industry standards, or a combination of both. Regulations should cover areas such as data privacy, algorithmic transparency, and the efficacy of AI-driven interventions.

Industry standards could also be critical in ensuring quality and consistency across different products. For instance, a certification process could be established where mental health technologies are independently assessed and certified based on their adherence to ethical and clinical standards. This would help build trust in these technologies and ensure their responsible use.

Holding Developers Accountable

Holding developers accountable for the performance and impact of their technologies is another crucial aspect of regulation. Developers should be required to conduct thorough testing and validation of their products before they are released to the public. Additionally, there should be mechanisms in place for ongoing monitoring and evaluation, allowing for the identification and correcting of any issues that arise after the product is launched.

Conclusion

Integrating technology into mental health care offers exciting possibilities but also brings significant ethical challenges. Privacy, algorithmic bias, and the potential erosion of the human element in care are just a few of the issues that must be addressed as we move forward. By prioritising ethical considerations and working to ensure that technology enhances rather than detracts from mental health care, we can create a future where these tools are used to their full potential, benefiting everyone in need of support.

As mental health technologies continue to evolve, it will be essential to maintain a focus on the principles that have always underpinned effective care: empathy, trust, and a deep understanding of the individual. By combining these principles with the capabilities of advanced technology, we can build a mental health care system that is both innovative and compassionate, serving the needs of all individuals with the care and respect they deserve.

Embracing a Holistic Approach to Mental Health

Introduction

Mental health is complex and multifaceted, influenced by biological, psychological, social, and environmental factors. A holistic approach recognises this complexity and seeks to address the whole person rather than focusing solely on symptoms. Understanding the importance of a holistic approach for young adults and parents can lead to more effective and sustainable mental health strategies. This chapter explores the principles of holistic mental health care, highlighting the interconnectedness of mind, body, and environment and offering practical strategies for achieving balance and well-being.

The Pillars of Holistic Mental Health

A holistic approach to mental health is built on several key pillars, each of which plays a vital role in overall well-being:

1. Physical Health: The connection between physical and mental health is well-established. Regular exercise, a balanced diet, adequate sleep, and proper medical care are essential components of mental well-being. Physical activity, in particular, has been shown to reduce symptoms of depression and anxiety, improve mood, and increase overall life satisfaction. Exercise stimulates the release of endorphins—natural mood lifters—and can also reduce levels of the stress hormone cortisol. Additionally, a nutritious diet that includes essential vitamins and minerals supports brain health, helping to regulate mood and cognitive function. Adequate sleep is another cornerstone of mental health, as it allows the brain to rest and recover, processes emotions, and supports cognitive functions such as memory and problem-solving.

2. Emotional Health: Emotional well-being involves understanding, managing, and expressing feelings in a healthy way. This includes developing coping strategies for dealing with stress, building resilience, and maintaining healthy relationships. Practices like mindfulness and meditation can enhance emotional health by promoting self-awareness and reducing emotional reactivity. Mindfulness, for instance, encourages individuals to stay present and observe their thoughts without judgment, which can reduce anxiety and prevent rumination. Emotional health also involves recognising and addressing underlying emotional issues, such as unresolved grief or trauma, that may be contributing to mental health challenges.

3. Social Health: Social connections are crucial for mental health. Supportive relationships with family, friends, and the broader community provide a sense of belonging and purpose. Social health also involves effective communication, setting boundaries, and engaging in meaningful social activities. Strong social networks can act as a buffer against stress, providing emotional support during difficult times. Conversely, social isolation is a significant risk factor for mental health problems, including depression and anxiety. Engaging in group activities, volunteering, or simply spending time with loved ones can enhance social health and improve overall well-being.

4. Environmental Health: The environment we live, work, and play in can significantly impact mental health. This includes both the physical environment — such as access to nature, clean air, and safe living conditions — and the social environment, including workplace culture, community support, and societal norms. Creating environments that promote safety, inclusivity, and well-being is crucial to holistic mental health. For example, access to green spaces has been shown to reduce stress and improve mood, while a supportive workplace environment can enhance job satisfaction and reduce burnout. Environmental health also involves reducing exposure to harmful substances, such as pollution and toxins, which can negatively impact mental health.

5. Spiritual Health: For many people, spirituality is an essential aspect of mental health. This can involve religious practices, a connection to something greater than oneself, or a commitment to personal values and purpose. Spiritual health contributes to a sense of meaning in life and can provide comfort and resilience in times of stress. Practices such as prayer, meditation, or spending time in nature can nurture spiritual health and promote inner peace. Additionally, engaging in activities that align with one's values and beliefs can foster a sense of purpose and fulfilment, which are important components of overall well-being.

Case Study: Holistic Mental Health in Practice

Consider the case of Mia, a 20-year-old college student who began experiencing symptoms of anxiety and depression during her second year of studies. Traditional therapy and medication provided some relief, but Mia found that her symptoms persisted. Her therapist suggested a more holistic approach, incorporating elements of physical, emotional, social, environmental, and spiritual health into her treatment plan.

Mia began by focusing on improving her physical health, incorporating regular exercise and a healthier diet into her routine. She found that jogging in the mornings not only boosted her mood but also improved her concentration throughout the day. Additionally, Mia made a conscious effort to prioritise sleep, establishing a bedtime routine that helped her get the rest she needed.

To address her emotional health, Mia started practising mindfulness and meditation. She set aside time each day to meditate, which helped her manage her anxiety and develop a greater sense of inner calm. Mia also worked on recognising and expressing her emotions, allowing herself to feel and process her feelings rather than suppressing them.

Recognising the importance of social connections, Mia made an effort to reconnect with friends and build a supportive network on campus. She joined a student group focused on mental health awareness, where she found camaraderie and understanding from others who shared similar experiences. This social support became a vital part of her recovery, providing her with a sense of belonging and reducing her feelings of isolation.

Mia also took steps to create a more peaceful living environment. She added plants to her dorm room, which brought a touch of nature indoors and helped create a calming atmosphere. She also sought out quiet spaces on campus where she could study and reflect without distractions.

Finally, Mia explored her spiritual health by reconnecting with her values and setting aside time for reflection and self-care. She began journaling about her experiences and contemplating her purpose and goals in life. This spiritual exploration gave Mia a deeper sense of meaning and direction, helping her navigate her challenges more resiliently.

Over time, these holistic changes led to a significant improvement in Mia's mental health. Mia achieved a greater sense of balance and well-being by addressing the whole person rather than just her symptoms.

Practical Strategies for Embracing a Holistic Approach

For those looking to embrace a holistic approach to mental health, here are some practical strategies:

1. Incorporate Regular Exercise: Find a form of physical activity you enjoy and make it a regular part of your routine. Regular exercise, whether it's yoga, running, or dancing, can profoundly impact your mental health. Even small amounts of physical activity, such as a daily walk, can help reduce stress and improve mood.

2. Practice Mindfulness and Meditation: Set aside time daily to practice mindfulness or meditation. These practices can help you manage stress, increase self-awareness, and improve emotional health. Mindfulness exercises, such as deep breathing or body scans, can be easily incorporated into your daily routine, even during moments of stress.

3. Build Strong Social Connections: Nurture your relationships with family and friends. Make time for social activities that bring joy and connect you with others. Whether it's sharing a meal with a loved one, joining a club, or volunteering, social interactions can provide emotional support and enrich your life.

4. Create a Positive Environment: Create a living and working environment that supports your mental health. This might involve decluttering, adding elements of nature, or creating spaces for relaxation and reflection.

Consider your environment's impact on your well-being and make changes promoting peace and security.

5. Explore Your Spiritual Health: Reflect on your values, purpose, and sense of meaning in life. Nurturing your spiritual health can contribute to overall well-being, whether through religious practices, personal reflection, or connection with nature. Engage in activities aligning with your beliefs and bringing you closer to your purpose.

Conclusion

A holistic approach to mental health recognises the interconnectedness of mind, body, and environment. By addressing all aspects of well-being, individuals can achieve greater balance and resilience, leading to more effective and sustainable mental health outcomes. For young adults and parents, embracing a holistic approach offers a comprehensive strategy for supporting mental health in a complex and ever-changing world.

This approach encourages us to look beyond symptoms and consider the broader context of our lives, recognising that mental health is influenced by various factors that must be addressed together. Doing so can create a more balanced, fulfilling, and healthy life, ensuring that our well-being is nurtured and supported.

Case Studies in AI and Trauma-Informed Mental Health Care

Introduction

The intersection of Artificial Intelligence (AI) and Trauma-Informed Care (TIC) represents one of the most promising advancements in modern mental health care. By combining the analytical power of AI with the empathetic, individualised approach of TIC, mental health professionals can offer more precise, effective, and compassionate care to those who have experienced trauma. This chapter delves into several detailed case studies illustrating how these two fields are integrated in practical settings. These examples highlight AI-enhanced Trauma-Informed Care's successes, challenges, and future possibilities.

Case Study 1: AI-Assisted Therapy for PTSD

Context and Background

Post-Traumatic Stress Disorder (PTSD) is a debilitating condition that affects millions worldwide, often resulting from experiences such as military combat, assault, accidents, or natural disasters. Traditional therapies for PTSD, including Cognitive Behavioural Therapy (CBT) and Exposure Therapy, are effective but can be challenging for those who find it difficult to revisit their trauma in therapy sessions.

Implementation of AI in Therapy

In recent years, AI has been integrated into PTSD treatment to enhance the therapeutic process. One notable application is the use of AI to monitor and analyse a patient's non-verbal cues — such as facial expressions, body language, and voice tone — during therapy sessions. This data is then used to provide real-time feedback to the therapist, helping them adjust their approach to meet the patient's needs more effectively.

Specific Example: The Case of Mark

Mark, a 32-year-old military veteran, struggled with severe PTSD after his return from active duty. He had participated in traditional therapy sessions but found it challenging to express his emotions and recount his experiences. The introduction of an AI-assisted therapy program changed the course of his treatment. The AI system monitored his sessions and could detect when Mark was overwhelmed — even when he could not verbalise it.

For instance, during a particularly intense session, the AI detected a subtle increase in Mark's heart rate and changes in his voice pitch, indicating rising anxiety. The system alerted the therapist, who then adjusted the session's pace, allowing Mark to take breaks and regain composure. Over time, this tailored approach helped Mark build trust and gradually process his trauma, leading to a significant reduction in his PTSD symptoms.

Outcomes and Lessons Learned

The use of AI in Mark's therapy sessions not only improved the effectiveness of his treatment but also highlighted the importance of integrating technology with human care. The AI provided insights the therapist might have missed, enabling a more nuanced and supportive therapeutic environment. However, this case also underscores the need for ongoing human oversight, as the therapist's role in interpreting AI data and providing empathetic care remained crucial. The balance between technology and human interaction is vital for maintaining the therapeutic relationship, which is central to successful PTSD treatment.

Case Study 2: Trauma-Informed AI in School Settings

Context and Background

Trauma among students, particularly those in middle and high school, is a growing concern. Many students experience adverse childhood experiences (ACEs), such as domestic violence, abuse, or community violence, which can significantly impact their academic performance and mental health. Schools are increasingly turning to AI to help identify and support these students.

Implementation of AI in Schools

In a pioneering programme at a middle school in Chicago, AI technology was integrated into the school's existing digital learning platform. The AI system was designed to monitor students' interactions with educational content and social interactions within the school's online environment. By analysing this data, the AI could detect patterns indicative of trauma-related issues, such as sudden drops in academic performance, withdrawal from social interactions, or changes in communication styles.

Specific Example: The Case of Emily

Emily, a 13-year-old student, had recently experienced a traumatic event at home. Although she continued to attend school, her grades began to slip, and she became increasingly isolated from her peers. The AI system flagged these changes and alerted the school's mental health team.

The school's counsellor, trained in Trauma-Informed Care, approached Emily non-intrusively, offering her a safe space to discuss her experiences. Over the following weeks, Emily received tailored support, including counselling sessions and adjustments to her academic workload to reduce stress. The early intervention made possible by the AI system prevented Emily's situation from escalating and helped her begin the healing process.

Outcomes and Lessons Learned

Emily's case demonstrates the potential of AI to act as an early warning system in educational settings, enabling timely and trauma-informed interventions. However, it also highlights the importance of training staff in TIC principles, as the effectiveness of AI interventions depends heavily on the human response. Additionally, this case underscores the need for transparency with students and parents about how AI is used, ensuring that privacy and ethical concerns are adequately addressed. Schools must balance the benefits of AI with the need to protect students' rights and foster a supportive educational environment.

Case Study 3: AI-Powered Trauma Support in Refugee Communities

Context and Background

Refugee populations often face significant trauma both in their countries of origin and during their resettlement. Traditional mental health services may not be easily accessible due to language barriers, cultural differences, or a lack of resources. AI-powered tools offer a promising solution to bridge these gaps and provide trauma-informed support to these vulnerable populations.

Implementation of AI in Refugee Care

An AI-powered mobile app was introduced in a refugee camp in Jordan to provide mental health support to Syrian refugees. The app was designed to assess users' mental health needs based on their interactions with it, including self-reported data, language use, and emotional tone. It offered culturally relevant resources such as guided meditations, relaxation exercises, and connections to local support services.

Specific Example: The Case of Ahmed

Ahmed, a 40-year-old refugee, had experienced significant trauma before fleeing Syria. He suffered from anxiety and depression but was hesitant to seek help due to language barriers and the stigma associated with mental health issues in his community. The AI-powered app, available in Arabic, allowed Ahmed to access mental health support privately.

The app's AI system identified patterns in Ahmed's usage that suggested he was at risk of worsening depression. It provided personalised resources, including breathing exercises and mindfulness practices, and encouraged him to seek further help from a local clinic. The app also facilitated a referral, making it easier for Ahmed to access in-person counselling when ready.

Outcomes and Lessons Learned

Ahmed's experience illustrates how AI-powered tools can overcome barriers to mental health care in refugee communities. The app provided a culturally sensitive, accessible, and trauma-informed approach to care, which helped Ahmed manage his symptoms and eventually seek further treatment. However, this case also highlights the importance of ensuring that AI tools are designed with cultural competence and integrated with local healthcare systems to provide comprehensive support. The success of such initiatives depends on understanding and respecting the unique needs of refugee populations and providing ongoing support and resources.

Challenges and Future Directions

While these case studies demonstrate the potential of AI and TIC, they also reveal challenges that must be addressed as these technologies evolve. Ensuring that AI systems are culturally sensitive, ethically sound, and free from bias is critical to their success. For instance, AI systems must be trained on diverse datasets to avoid perpetuating existing biases and inequalities in mental health care.

Moreover, integrating AI with human care requires ongoing training for professionals to interpret and act on AI-generated insights effectively. As AI becomes more prevalent in mental health settings, it will be essential for mental health professionals to receive training on how to use these tools effectively while maintaining the human touch, which is crucial for trauma-informed care.

The future of AI-enhanced Trauma-Informed Care will likely involve more sophisticated algorithms, greater integration with existing mental health systems, and broader accessibility across different populations. For example, advancements in natural language processing and machine learning could enable AI systems to understand better and respond to the nuanced emotional states of individuals. As these technologies continue to develop, they promise to make mental health care more personalised, effective, and compassionate.

Conclusion

The integration of AI with Trauma-Informed Care has the potential to revolutionise mental health treatment, offering more nuanced, effective, and accessible care for those who have experienced trauma. The case studies presented in this chapter provide a glimpse into how these technologies are applied in real-world settings, demonstrating their potential and the challenges that must be addressed. As we continue to explore and refine these approaches, AI and TIC will likely become central components of a more responsive and humane mental health care system.

By harnessing the power of AI while remaining grounded in the principles of Trauma-Informed Care, mental health professionals can offer innovative solutions that respect and enhance the human experience. The future of mental health care will depend on our ability to integrate these technologies thoughtfully, ensuring they are used to support and empower those in need of care.

The Path Forward: Preparing for the Future of Mental Health Care

Introduction

The mental health landscape is rapidly evolving, driven by advances in technology, a growing understanding of mental health issues, and an increasing demand for personalised care. As we look to the future, it is crucial to consider how these changes will impact individuals, families, and communities. This chapter explores the key trends and developments likely to shape the future of mental health care, offering insights into how we can prepare for these changes. It discusses the implications for young adults, parents, and mental health professionals, emphasising the need for adaptability, advocacy, and resilience.

Emerging Trends in Mental Health Care

1. Personalised Mental Health Care

The future of mental health care is increasingly moving towards personalisation, where treatment plans are tailored to each individual's unique needs, preferences, and life circumstances. AI plays a central role in this trend by analysing large datasets to identify patterns and predict which interventions will most likely succeed for each person.

For example, an AI-driven mental health platform might analyse data from a person's genetic profile, medical history, and daily behaviour to recommend a specific combination of therapy, medication, and lifestyle changes. This level of personalisation can lead to more effective treatments and better outcomes, as interventions are tailored to the individual rather than relying on a one-size-fits-all approach. Moreover, personalised care can adapt over time, responding to changes in an individual's life circumstances or mental health status, thereby providing ongoing, dynamic support.

2. Teletherapy and Virtual Care

The COVID-19 pandemic accelerated the adoption of teletherapy and virtual mental health services, a trend likely to continue and evolve. Teletherapy offers the convenience of receiving care from home, making it easier for individuals with busy schedules, mobility issues, or those living in remote areas to access mental health services. As technology advances, we expect to see more sophisticated virtual care platforms incorporating AI, virtual reality (VR), and augmented reality (AR).

These technologies will allow therapists to create immersive environments for exposure therapy and simulate social scenarios, enhancing the effectiveness of treatments like Cognitive Behavioural Therapy (CBT). For instance, a person struggling with social anxiety could practice conversations in a virtual environment that mimics real-world interactions. This approach helps individuals build confidence and reduce stress in a safe, controlled setting before applying these skills in real-world situations. Additionally, teletherapy platforms may begin to offer more integrated services, combining therapy with other forms of support, such as digital self-help tools, peer support networks, and wellness resources.

3. Preventive Mental Health

Another significant trend shaping the future of mental health care is the shift towards prevention. Rather than focusing solely on treating mental health issues once they arise, there is a growing emphasis on identifying risk factors early and implementing interventions that can prevent the onset of mental illness. AI and machine learning are instrumental in this shift, as they can analyse vast amounts of data to identify individuals at risk of developing mental health conditions.

For instance, an AI system might monitor a person's social media activity, wearable device data, and even their communication patterns to detect early signs of depression or anxiety. If certain risk factors are identified, the system could prompt the individual to engage in preventive activities, such as practising mindfulness, seeking social support, or scheduling a session with a therapist. This proactive approach could significantly reduce the prevalence of mental health conditions and improve overall well-being. Moreover, preventive mental health strategies can be tailored to specific populations, such as adolescents, senior citizens, or individuals with a family history of mental illness, making them more effective and targeted.

4. Global Mental Health Initiatives

Mental health care is no longer confined to national borders. With the rise of digital platforms and global communication networks, mental health services are increasingly being delivered globally. This trend is significant for reaching underserved populations in low- and middle-income countries, where access to traditional mental health services may be limited.

Global mental health initiatives often leverage AI to provide scalable, culturally sensitive care. For example, AI-powered chatbots that offer mental health support in multiple languages can give immediate, accessible help to individuals worldwide. These initiatives often involve partnerships between governments, NGOs, and private companies to ensure that mental health services are available to those most in need. Additionally, these global initiatives may focus on building local capacity, training mental health professionals in culturally relevant approaches, and using technology to bridge gaps in service delivery.

Preparing for the Future

As these trends continue to shape the future of mental health care, it is essential to consider how individuals, families, and communities can prepare for these changes. Here are some key strategies:

1. Education and Awareness

Staying informed about the latest developments in mental health care is essential for everyone—whether you are a young adult navigating your mental health journey, a parent supporting a child, or a mental health professional. This includes understanding the benefits and limitations of new technologies and the ethical considerations they raise.

For parents, this might involve educating their children about the responsible use of mental health apps and other digital tools, ensuring they understand the importance of privacy and the potential risks associated with sharing personal information online. For professionals, ongoing education about the latest advancements in AI and virtual care is crucial to staying relevant and effective in a rapidly changing field. Educational initiatives could also extend to schools and communities, raising awareness about mental health and promoting the use of preventive and personalised care.

2. Embracing Change

Integrating technology into mental health care is inevitable; embracing these changes with an open mind will be vital to making the most of these innovations. This doesn't mean accepting all new technologies without question but being willing to explore how they can complement and enhance traditional approaches to care.

For individuals, this might involve experimenting with different digital tools to find those that best support their mental health. For mental health professionals, it means staying current with technological advancements and considering how they can be incorporated into their practice to serve their clients better. Embracing change also involves being adaptable and flexible, recognising that the landscape of mental health care is constantly evolving, and being open to new ways of thinking and working.

3. Advocating for Ethical Standards

As AI and other technologies become more prevalent in mental health care, there is a pressing need for clear ethical standards and regulations. This includes ensuring that these technologies protect privacy, prevent bias, and maintain the human element of care.

Advocating for ethical standards might involve supporting policies that regulate the use of AI in mental health care and ensuring that these technologies are developed and implemented in fair, transparent, and accountable ways. It also means being an informed consumer or professional, asking questions about how data is used, and advocating for practices that prioritise the well-being of individuals. Ethical advocacy can take many forms, from participating in professional organisations to engaging in public policy discussions and supporting research exploring new technologies' ethical implications.

4. Building Resilience

Mental health care is not just about treating conditions — it's also about building resilience. This involves developing coping strategies, fostering strong social connections, and maintaining a healthy lifestyle. Building resilience is especially important as we face the uncertainties and challenges of the future.

This might involve learning how to manage stress, developing healthy habits, and seeking supportive relationships for young adults. For parents, it might mean modelling resilience for their children, teaching them how to navigate challenges, and providing a stable, supportive environment. Mental health professionals can also play a key role in fostering resilience, both in their clients and in their communities, by promoting mental health education, advocating for supportive policies, and helping individuals build the skills they need to thrive in a changing world.

Case Study: A Vision for the Future

Let's imagine a scenario that encapsulates the future of mental health care:

Alex, a 24-year-old graduate student, has been experiencing early signs of depression. Recognising the need for support, Alex downloads an AI-powered mental health app that integrates personalised care with the latest advancements in AI technology. The app tracks Alex's mood, sleep patterns, and daily activities, providing customised recommendations based on this data.

Through the app, Alex connects with a therapist via teletherapy sessions, during which the therapist uses virtual reality to simulate stressful situations in a controlled environment. This helps Alex practice real-time coping strategies, which can be applied in real-world scenarios. The app also monitors Alex's progress and adjusts the treatment plan as needed, ensuring that the care remains personalised and effective.

Throughout this process, Alex's data is protected by robust encryption, and the AI system is regularly updated to ensure it remains free from bias. The app also provides Alex's family with resources to support Alex's mental health journey, creating a comprehensive support network.

This vision illustrates the potential future of mental health care — personalised, accessible, and ethically sound. As we move forward, the integration of AI, TIC, and other advanced technologies will play a pivotal role in shaping a mental health care system that is more inclusive, effective, and compassionate.

Conclusion

As we prepare for the future of mental health care, it is clear that technology will play an increasingly central role in shaping how we understand, treat, and prevent mental health conditions. By staying informed, embracing change, advocating for ethical standards, and building resilience, individuals, families, and mental health professionals can ensure that these advancements benefit everyone. The future of mental health care holds great promise, but it also requires careful consideration, thoughtful planning, and a commitment to the well-being of all.

As these innovations continue to develop, we must remain vigilant in ensuring that they are used to enhance, rather than replace, the human element of care. By combining the power of technology with the compassion and empathy that are the hallmarks of effective mental health treatment, we can create a future where everyone has the opportunity to achieve mental well-being.